More Mad About Meyer Lemons

More Mad About Meyer Lemons

Written and illustrated by
A. Cort Sinnes

Hearth & Garden Productions

More Mad About Meyer Lemons
Third Edition (Updated and Expanded) 2026

Printed in the United States of America

This book was designed and produced by
Hearth & Garden Productions
A. Cort Sinnes, Text, Design and Illustrations

Sinnes, A. Cort
More Mad About Meyer Lemons,
written and illustrated by
A. Cort Sinnes

ISBN 979-8-234-00402-4

For Frank N. Meyer,
for all he did to make this a more
beautiful and delicious country

Table of Contents

Notes on the Third Edition

I published the original *Mad About Meyer Lemons* some ten-plus years ago. As one who was taken by this special citrus, I knew there must be others who would enjoy a book exploring the unique qualities of 'Meyer' lemons. Since that time the popularity of 'Meyer' lemons has continued to increase as more gardeners and home cooks discover their charms. I was reasonably pleased with the way the original edition turned out in 2015, but eleven years is a long time. About a year ago, I couldn't help but notice some of the paintings and recipes had begun to show their age, so I decided to do a major revision, which is what you are holding in your hands, namely *More Mad About Meyer Lemons.*

How did I come up with the idea more than a decade ago to paint 36 views of 'Meyer" lemons? Two artists, Katsushika Hokusai and Henri Rivière, worlds and generations apart, provided the inspiration. In 1820s Japan, Hokusai produced what he called *36 Views of Mt. Fuji*, including the very famous "Great Wave off Kanagawa," pictured at right. Inspired by Hokusai, some eighty years later in Paris, the artist Henri Rivière produced *36 Views of the Eiffel Tower* in 1902. To this day, reproductions of both the Mt. Fuji woodblock prints and the Eiffel Tower lithographs have continued to be immensely popular with the international art-loving public.

So, in the tradition of Hokusai and Rivière, I offer you 36 views of 'Meyer' lemons as companions to some very tasty, updated recipes. As a subject to paint, they never cease to amaze me—gems of the plant kingdom, each lemon its own bit of perfection, from one home garden to another.

Note: Although the recipes in this book call for 'Meyer' lemons, standard sour lemons can be substituted. The finished dishes will not have the special 'Meyer' magic, but will still be tasty and satisfying.

A. Cort Sinnes

Above: *The Great Wave off Kanagawa, Hokusai's most famous work.* Left: *Katsushika Hokusai* (1760–1849) *self-portrait.*

Above: *One of Rivière's 36 views of the Eiffel Tower. Note that it is still under construction.* Left: *Henri Rivière* (1864–1951).

Frank Nicholas Meyer
1875 - 1918

> I am pessimistic by nature, and have not found a road which leads to relaxation. I withdraw from humanity and try to find relaxation with plants. I live now in expectation of what will come.
>
> *Frank N. Meyer, from a 1901 letter to a friend*

Considering the name "Meyer" occurs in the title of this book, it only seems fair that some consideration is given to the remarkable life of the man known as Frank N. Meyer who, considering his achievements, is pretty much unsung these days. Although there's not a great deal out there about his life, I came away with the impression that Meyer was not only a loner, but occasionally lonely, and for all the plants he found, I'm not sure he ever discovered another human being he could celebrate. Not to mention that this is a guy who had to keep his work boots on when he slept so the rats wouldn't chew on his ankles—but more about that later.

We have this man, Frank Nicholas Meyer, to thank for finding the 'Meyer' lemon in China (circa 1909) and introducing it to the West.

Born Frans Nicholaas Meijer in Amsterdam in 1875, Meyer showed an early interest in plants, beginning his horticultural career at age 14 working as a gardener's helper at the Amsterdam Botanical Garden. Encouraged by the director of the garden, Meyer became proficient in French and English and studied botany at the University of Groningen. A natural wanderer, Meyer left the botanic garden to see the plants and gardens of western Europe for himself, setting off on foot to travel through Belgium, Germany, France, Switzerland, Italy and Spain.

After his pedestrian tour of western Europe, Meyer traveled to England where he worked a stint in a commercial nursery before hitting the road again, this time to America. He arrived in 1901 and, with the help of his old boss at the Amsterdam Botanical Garden, got a job with the United States Department of Agriculture. After only a year, he was ready for adventure again and set off on his own to explore the indigenous plants of Mexico, Cuba, and California, working in nurseries along the way to pay for his expenses.

Three years later, Meyer returned to the USDA where he caught the eye of the chairman of the Foreign Plant Introduction Section, David Fairchild, who recognized Meyer's potential as an Agricultural Explorer, Meyer's official title. Fairchild introduced Meyer to Charles Sprague, the director of Harvard's Arnold Arboretum. Fairchild and Sprague worked out an arrangement for Meyer to study and collect plants in the Far East. Sprague was primarily interested in ornamental plants of commercial interest to America's nursery trade; Fairchild was more interested in food crops. Together they schooled Meyer in what had already been discovered so he wouldn't duplicate previous exploration efforts. With that they sent him off on a 13-year odyssey—four separate trips, each lasting between two and three years—resulting in the introduction of approximately 2,500 species to American farmers, nurseries, and home gardeners, including the 'Meyer' lemon.

In reading through Fairchild's and Sprague's correspondence with Meyer, I have to say they worked him like a rented mule. Their individual "wish lists" were as long as they were specific—everything from opium poppy seeds (anticipating the increased need for morphine with the outbreak of World War I), to soybeans (virtually unknown in America), water chestnuts (ditto), to lilacs, apricots, crabapples, Chinese pistachios and persimmons and everything in between. At one dark point in his travels, a doctor diagnoses Meyer as having "nervous prostration." Meyer wrote to Fairchild in 1917:

> How long I myself will be able to travel about in China yet, I do not know, but it seems that I may return sooner than I expected, perhaps in 1918. The loneliness and the hardships of life here are beginning to be more and more distasteful to me and the time is approaching that I'll have to leave further exploration of China in the hands of younger men.

Fairchild, ever the task master, wasn't exactly supportive or understanding of what had to be for Meyer, a very difficult letter to write:

> If conditions stop your work you will of course cable me and we will arrange for your return to America. I hope they will allow you to go on exploring for we have only one life to live and we want to spend it enriching our own country with the plants of the world which produce good things to eat and to look at.

At various times, Meyer's journeys took him to Mongolia, Manchuria, Korea, Siberia, the Crimea, Azerbaijan, Armenia, Turkmenestan, Chinese Turkestan and Tibet, often during turbulent and dangerous political times when any foreigner was looked on with suspicion. Conditions were about as rough as can be imagined. In an April 16, 1917 letter to David Fairchild, Meyer makes one of his few complaints:

> In the mountains whole villages are syphilitic; people without noses are often met with and syphilitic blindness and deafness are very common. In the inns the vermin are exceedingly plentiful and bloodthirsty and ordinary travelers have to sleep three abreast in one bedstead or on one broad bench and the stinkingly dirty bedcovers are kept in use until they fall to pieces. No wonder that 80% of the population suffers from all sorts of skin diseases, being inoculated by lice, fleas and bedbugs. I slept most times with my hunting boots on, for the vermin bites one especially at one's feet and legs, having learned no doubt that they are less easily caught there.

On his fourth and final expedition to the Far East in 1918, Meyer died aboard a steamer headed for Shanghai. The next day his body was found in the Yangtze River. Whether he fell from the steamer, either accidentally or on purpose—or was pushed—is not known. In the common parlance, it is written that he died under "mysterious circumstances." He was 43 years old. He is buried in Shanghai.

> Our short life will never be long enough to find out all about this mighty land. When I think about all these unexplored areas, I get fairly dazzled; one will never be able to cover them all. I will have to roam around in my next life.
>
> *– Frank Meyer in a letter to David Fairchild, May, 1907*

What's in a Name?

In 1909, when Frank Meyer encountered in China what would eventually become known as the 'Meyer' lemon, it appears that it was almost as much of a novelty to the Chinese as it was to Meyer himself. At the time, it was grown almost exclusively in containers, indoors and out, and enjoyed as the highly ornamental plant it is—the fruit being seen almost as an afterthought. Researchers are in general agreement that it is a naturally-occuring hybrid (rather than a man-made cross between two species) and even though most articles on 'Meyer' lemons state that it's a cross between the more standard sour lemon and a mandarin orange, genetic work done at the University of California at Riverside has shown that it is, in fact, a cross between a lemon and an orange. The defining characteristics of a 'Meyer' lemon are its thin skin, comparatively sweet flavor (less acidic than a sour lemon), extreme juiciness and an almost perfumelike fragrance. After it had been introduced to the American gardening public, it remained something of a backyard curiosity as opposed to a commercial crop, owing to the fact that its thin skin made it almost impossible to ship any distance. And so, for all of its charms, the 'Meyer' lemon languished in home gardens for generations, primarily in Florida, Texas and California. It wasn't until two culinary mavens, Alice Waters and Martha Stewart, started singing its praises that the 'Meyer' lemon finally received greater recognition and an almost cult status. With its new-found fame, the 'Meyer' lemon finally began showing up in grocery stores across the country during its rather short season of availability between between December and March, introducing a new generation to the pleasures of this unique citrus. Somewhere, Frank Meyer should be taking a well-deserved and long overdue bow.

In areas of the country too cold for the 'Meyer' lemon, it performs admirably well in containers indoors, just as it did when Frank Meyer originally found it in China more than 100 years ago.

Throughout the far west, Texas and Florida, 'Meyer' lemons are so ubiquitous in home gardens that they are almost taken for granted. What the rest of the country wouldn't give to have these delicious beauties right outside their back doors!

'MEYER' LIMONANA

Limonana is very popular throughout the Middle East. Not surprising, there are lots of variations and I'm here to put one more twist on it, namely making it with 'Meyer' lemons, which is very good, indeed. The first time I tried the standard version, I was with my daughter in a Middle Eastern restaurant in Berkeley. She was very familiar with it, but it was completely new to me—minty, green lemonade—who knew? It's not meant to be overly sweet, so the natural sweetness of the 'Meyer' lemon comes as an added benefit here. If you're feeling particularly frisky, add a shot of gin or vodka to the mix. Serves two.

1 cup 'Meyer' lemon juice, approximately 7 or 8 lemons
½ cup roughly-torn or chopped fresh mint
1 cup water
4 tablespoons granulated sugar
2 cups ice cubes
Fresh mint sprigs for garnish

Put all ingredients in a blender and blend at high speed until the ice is well crushed. Serve in tall glasses, garnished with fresh mint sprigs.

Gardeners who have never grown 'Meyer' lemons before are astounded at the size of the crop these relatively small trees and shrubs can produce. Luckily the fruits last for months on the plants and can be harvested over time.

‘MEYER’ LEMON COOLER WITH PROSECCO

Back in the day, some dubious ale was marketed as “a lot to drink without drinking a lot.” Well, this is just the opposite: light in every sense of the word, refreshing and non-fillling. A great hot weather drink, or for when you’ve been designated the driver.

Prosecco, well-chilled
Club soda, cold
1 teaspoon ‘Meyer’ lemon juice
‘Meyer’ lemon peel, cut like a curled ribbon
Cracked ice

Fill a large, tall glass (a pilsner glass is best) with cracked ice. Pour the ‘Meyer’ lemon juice over the ice. Slowly fill the glass about two-thirds full with prosecco. Top with the club soda and give it a quick stir. Rub the rim of the glass with the ‘Meyer’ lemon ribbon and leave as a garnish.

I purchased this cocktail shaker from the estate of Laurence Sickman, longtime Curator of Oriental Art at the Nelson-Atkins Museum in Kansas City, where he assembled one of the great collections of Asisan art in the world. Made in China of Chinese silver, it seems right at home with Frank Meyer's lemons.

PORTUGUESE SCOTCH SOUR

Way back when, sometime in the 1970s when whiskey sours were far more popular than they are now, a sophisticated friend of mine introduced me to this drink. She had spent time in Portugal and told me they were all the rage there. True or not, this is a delicious drink, especially if you're a Scotch drinker. Perfect during hot weather, but watch out: they go down so easy you may find yourself being taken home in a wheelbarrow.

2 ounces Scotch whisky
Juice of ½ 'Meyer' lemon
1 teaspoon superfine sugar
Mint sprig for garnish, if desired

Put whisky, lemon juice and sugar in a cocktail shaker about half-filled with ice cubes. Shake vigorously. Strain into a chilled cocktail glass. Garnish with a sprig of mint. Fasten your seatbelt...

Having the right glass for a particular drink may be going the way of the dodo bird, but back in the day, it would have been unthinkable to serve a Tom Collins in anything other than a tall, skinny "Collins glass."

'MEYER' LEMON TOM COLLINS

Although the traditional Tom Collins cocktail is made with gin, as you can see in the illustration, I prefer mine made with vodka. Pick your poison, as they say. The nice thing about building your own Tom Collins is that you can adjust the sweetness to your own preference; for me, the less sweet it is, the more refreshing its effect. It has been popular since the mid-1800s, when it was described as "gin and sparkling lemonade," which is exactly what it is. A "Collins glass" is taller and narrower than a standard highball glass and is considered de rigueur for serving this classic cocktail.

2 ounces vodka (or gin)
1 teaspoon superfine sugar
½ ounce 'Meyer' lemon juice
Club soda
Thin 'Meyer' lemon wedge
Sprig of fresh mint

Combine vodka, sugar and lemon juice in a Collins glass three-quarters full of cracked ice. Stir briefly, top with club soda or seltzer, garnish with lemon slice and spring of mint and serve with a stirring rod.

It really is as if 'Meyer' lemons are filled with sunshine, glowing from within—at least that was my intent with this painting: a slice lit from the inside.

'MEYER' LEMON LIMONCELLO

Bright and refreshing, limoncello is wonderful as a palate cleanser, especially as an after-dinner drink served icy-cold, straight, in a chilled shot glass. It is an incomparable digestive; mixed with tonic water it is a sweet, tasty refreshment. It's also great with champagne or mixed with juice as a cocktail. This recipe is courtesy of Everclear—yes, that very high octane liquor more commonly known as "white lightning." That said, they know a thing or two about making an excellent limoncello.

10 'Meyer' lemons, peels only (avoid the white pith)
One (750-ml) bottle Everclear
3½ cups water
2½ cups granulated sugar

1. Using a sharp vegetable peeler, peel ten freshly washed, organic lemons, leaving as much of the white pith behind as possible. If there's pith still left on the peels, lay them peel side down and scrape the pith away using a sharp paring knife. If left on, the pith will cause the limoncello to be bitter.

2. Combine lemon zest and Everclear in a large, sealable container, at least two quarts in size. Let steep for at least four days and up to four weeks in a cool, dry place.

3. After the lemon-Everclear mixture is infused to your liking, combine sugar and water in a medium saucepan. Bring to a boil, stirring regularly until sugar is fully dissolved, approximately 5-10 minutes. Let syrup cool to room temperature. Add the simple syrup to the lemon infusion gradually, tasting as you go, until it has the level of sweetness you desire.

4. Strain mixture through a fine mesh stainer. Pour into smaller bottles and chill in freezer. Enjoy.

It continues to amaze me that 'Meyer' lemons are at the absolute height of their glory in the darkest days of winter. Their beauty, fragrance and flavor brighten many a kitchen counter on a gloomy winter day.

'MEYER' LEMON INFUSED OLIVE OIL

If you like to cook, you've no doubt run across some of the outstanding infused olive oils out there, including 'Meyer' lemon. If you have a 'Meyer' lemon tree, you are no doubt also aware of how prolific they are. This "recipe" is the essence of simplicity and is a good one for using plenty of lemons, especially is you make extra infused oil to give as special gifts—any time of the year. The peel is what you use for this process; the leftover flesh can be juiced and frozen in ice cube trays for use later. Once solidly frozen, put the juice cubes in zippered plastic storage bags and keep frozen until needed.

2 cups extra virgin olive oil
Peels from 4 'Meyer' lemon (avoid the bitter white pith)

1. Wash lemons and pat them dry.

2. Carefully peel the lemons using a vegetable peeler or paring knife; you want the yellow part only, leaving the white pithy layer on the lemon.

3. In a medium saucepan, combine the olive oil and lemon peels.

4. Warm the oil over low heat for about 15-20 minutes. The goal is to just gently warm the oil and peels. Do not allow to reach a simmer or boil (keep the temperature below 150°F). Overheating can change the oil's flavor.

5. After 20 minutes, remove the pan from the heat and allow to cool and steep for 45 minutes to an hour. The longer it steeps, the stronger the flavor will be.

6. Strain the oil through a fine-mesh strainer or cheesecloth into a clean, sterilized glass jar or bottle, discarding the peels. Store in a cool, dark place or in the refrigerator for up to a month. If refrigerated, the oil might solidify; simply run the bottle under warm water before use.

Preserved 'Meyer' lemons are so easy to prepare—and such an important and distinctive addition to so many dishes—you owe it to yourself to make some right away. French Hermitique jars, with their rubber seals and heavy wire bails, are ideal containers for this exotic treat. Preserved lemons last practically forever if kept in the refrigerator.

MOROCCAN PRESERVED 'MEYER' LEMONS

As exotic as Moroccan perserved lemons sounds, they are very easy to make at home. If you have a bumper crop, as so many people do, make several jars and give as special gifts. Nothing else tastes quite like preserved 'Meyer' lemons; once you start using them, you'll be hooked. Be advised they are very salty; most people lightly rinse them in cold water and blot them dry before using. Most recipes use the rind only, not the flesh.

6 to 7 'Meyer' lemons
¼ cup salt
8 black peppercorns
1 bay leaf
1 whole dried red pepper (optional)
Extra lemons for juice

1 sterilized half-liter jar

1. Put one tablespoon of the salt into the bottom of the jar. Cut the lemons into quarters, from the top down, leaving the bottom ½-inch of the lemon still joined as one. Sprinkle salt on the exposed flesh and press into lemons. Pack the lemons tightly into the jar, adding the peppercorns, bay leaf, and red pepper (if desired) as you go, and more salt evenly between layers.

2. If the juice produced by packing them into the jar isn't enough to cover them, add more lemon juice until they are submerged. Leave a little airspace at the top and seal the jar.

3. Store the jar at room temperature for 30 days, shaking the jar occasionally. After 30 days, store the preserved lemons in the refrigerator.

A row of sunshine and goodness. 'Meyer' lemon marmalade lined up on the windowsill. Wonderful to give as gifts during the winter holidays.

'MEYER' LEMON MARMALADE

My friend, Patty, who has a 'Meyer' lemon bush as big as a Volkswagen right outside her kitchen window, came up with this recipe. It's the essence of simplicity and delicious, just as it is. The late Nan McEvoy, founder of the McEvoy Ranch in Petaluma (known for its world-class olive oils), suggested combining 'Meyer' lemon marmalade with soy sauce as glaze for broiled salmon. Sounds good to me. Yields three to four half-pint jars.

4 'Meyer' lemons, very thinly sliced, seeds removed
4 cups water
4 cups granulated sugar

1. After the lemons have been thinly sliced and the seeds removed, roughly chop them. You should have about two cups. Put four cups of water in a heavy sauce pan over medium-high heat. Bring to a boil and add the chopped lemons. Boil gently for 30 to 40 minutes, until the chopped lemons have softened.

2. Add the sugar and increase heat under the pan. Bring mixture to a boil, stirring constantly, until the mixture registers 220°F on a candy thermometer.

3. Allow to cool slightly and then pour into sterilized jars. Marmalade can be processed in a hot water bath, according to the canning jar manufacturer's instructions, to achieve a vacuum seal. Any jars that don't seal properly should be refrigerated and used within 2 to 4 weeks.

For all their good qualities, it’s easy to elevate ‘Meyer’ lemons. They seem right at home placed on silver pedestal.

STEWED PRUNES WITH 'MEYER' LEMONS

I know this is going to be a tough sell, especially with a name as unappealing as "stewed prunes," but I urge you to give it a try because stewed prunes are truly delicious and, when accented as they are here with the flavor of 'Meyer' lemons, have a complex and appealing flavor. And, of course, as everyone seems to know, prunes are good for you. I didn't have a chance to develop an automatic dislike for this dish because my Scandinavian grandmother started serving them to me when I was a kid. Different cultures add red wine, orange slices, cinnamon sticks and/or a vanilla bean to the mix; personally I prefer the simplicity of lemon slices only. Straight from the refrigerator, thoroughly chilled, sweet and syrupy, with a lemony spark, what's not to like?

1 pound whole, pitted prunes (non-sorbate, if available)
1 'Meyer' lemon, cut into ¼-inch slices
Water

1. Combine the prunes and lemon slices in a medium saucepan; add water to just cover prunes. Cover with a lid and cook over medium-low heat. Allow to just simmer, approximately 25 minutes. Cool.

2. Cover and store in the refrigerator for up to a month. Serve plain for a breakfast treat, or as an after-dinner dessert topped with mascarpone or a crunchy cookie on the side, or both. Also particularly good on hot breakfast cereal or vanilla ice cream.

The blossoms on 'Meyer' lemon plants start out an unusual shade of violet, which combined with the yellow of the lemons constitute a classic pair of "complementary" colors—meaning they are directly opposite each other on a color wheel. Seen together they create a strong visual contrast, making each color stand out more.

NAPA CABBAGE 'MEYER' LEMON COLESLAW

I'm not sure how this variation of coleslaw came into being, but I'm glad it did. I've never been a big fan of slaw until I started adding Napa cabbage to the mix. I really like its softer texture and the almost complete lack of sulphur odor so characteristic of most cabbages. Since I was starting with an Asian vein, I just kept with it, resulting in this "not your grandmother's coleslaw." Makes four to six servings.

3 cups Napa cabbage, shredded (or, if you want a slaw with a little more "tooth" to it, us one-half shredded Napa cabbage and one-half shredded regular cabbage)
4 chopped green onions, white and green parts
⅓ cup fresh cilantro, chopped
½ large carrot, shredded
1 fresh jalapeño chile, seeds removed, diced (optional)
1 tablespoon toasted sesame seeds
Juice of one 'Meyer' lemon
1½ teaspoons mirin (substitute ½ teaspoon of granulated sugar if you don't have mirin)
1 tablespoon toasted sesame oil
2 tablespoons rice wine vinegar

1. Place the shredded cabbage, green onions, cilantro, shredded carrots, optional jalapeño chiles and toasted sesame seeds in a large bowl. Toss lightly to mix ingredients.

2. Make the dressing by combining lemon juice, mirin, toasted sesame oil and rice vinegar in a small bowl, whisking it with a fork. Pour over the slaw ingredients and toss thoroughly. Refrigerate for 30 minutes or so to allow the flavors to "marry." Be prepared to like slaw, even if you never have before.

This is what 'Meyer' lemons look like in autumn, before they ripen in time for the winter holidays. Evergreen 'Meyer' lemons are truly plants that are beautiful year 'round.

CRISPY NEW POTATOES WITH MISO 'MEYER' MAYONNAISE

I'm not going to enter the fray as to whether it was the Belgians or the French who invented "french fries," but I know for certain that the Belgians love the combination of french fries and mayonnaise. This dish was inspired by one I ran across on Food 52, *the excellent food blog found on the internets machine. I tweaked it a bit and I'm here to tell you it's some kind of wonderful. Try them once and I guarantee they'll become a favorite. Makes four servings.*

1½ pounds new potatoes
¼ cup mayonnaise
2 teaspoons miso paste (brown is best)
Juice and zest of ½ 'Meyer' lemon
Oil for frying (olive oil preferred)
2 green onions, trimmed and thinly sliced
Salt and freshly ground pepper, to taste

1. Scrub the potatoes and place on a steamer in a pot with a lid. Bring water to a boil, cover pot, and reduce to a simmer. Start checking potatoes after eight minutes. They're done when the tip of sharp knife penetrates the potato easily.

2. While the potatoes cook, spray or wipe a large platter with oil. Spread the cooked potatoes on the platter; let them sit for five minutes to cool slightly.

3. Mix the mayonnaise, miso, and lemon juice and zest thoroughly in a small bowl. Store in refrigerator until ready to use.

4. When the potatoes are cool enough to touch, gently smash/flatten them with the heel of your hand or press with a sturdy spatula. Try to keep them from breaking into pieces.

5. In a skillet, fry the potatoes in about ¼-inch of olive oil over medium-high heat until the edges start to brown, about 4 to 5 minutes or so per side. Once done, drizzle liberally with the miso mayonnaise and sprinkle the chopped green onions. Serve hot, directly from the skillet.

Normally filled with paintbrushes, I decided to fill this unusual blue-and-white "pencil jar" with mustard flowers and pair it with another late winter speciality, a ripe 'Meyer' lemon. Many shades of yellow during the dark time of year.

AVOCADO TOAST, TWO WAYS

Given its rise and fall (and seeming rise again) in the digital realm, the origins of avocado toast go back much further in time than you might expect—like to the 1920s. It's one of those things so simple and fundamentally good—like peanut butter on toast or cream cheese on a bagel—that it should just be taken for the bit of goodness it is and leave it at that. In its purest form (see Version One, below), spread half an avocado on a piece of good quality toast, smash it evenly with a fork, squeeze a little 'Meyer' lemon juice over the top and sprinkle with salt and chile pepper flakes to taste. A satisfying way to start the day or as an after-school snack. My friend Amy tweaked it in her inimitable style and offers Version Two, below.

Version One:
A slice good quality bread, toasted
½ avocado
Squeeze of fresh 'Meyer' lemon juice, to taste
Salt, to taste
Dried chile flakes, to taste

1. Toast bread to desired doneness.

2. Mash avocado in a bowl or directly on the slice of toast; squeeze 'Meyer' lemon juice over top and sprinkle with salt and dried chile pepper flakes, to taste.

Version Two:
A slice good quality bread, toasted
½ avocado
Coarsely chopped tomato, roughly the same amount as the avocado
Squeeze of fresh 'Meyer' lemon juice, to taste
Salt, to taste
Your favorite Chili Crisp, to taste, about a tablespoon
Mayonnaise, about a tablespoon

1. Combine all ingredients and spread on toast. Drizzle a little quality olive oil over the top. Eat over the sink. Delish!

Even cutting just one 'Meyer' lemon in half is quite the sensory experience—pleasing the eyes, the nose, and your taste buds.

BABA GHANOUSH ON THE GRILL

We all know that grilling is part culinary theater; cooking a whole eggplant that puffs up like one those foil turbans filled with popcorn from days of yore, definitely adds a performative aspect to this excellent recipe. Makes four modest servings. Here's what you need and how to do it on a gas grill:

One large eggplant (about a pound)
Olive oil
Juice of one-half 'Meyer' lemon
¼ cup tahini
Pressed garlic, to taste
Ground cumin, to taste
Salt and freshly ground pepper
Chopped fresh parsley and chopped toasted walnuts, for garnish
Serve with warm slices of rustic bread or pita triangles

1. Preheat the grill with all the burners on high and the lid closed for ten minutes.

2. Turn all the burners to medium. Place the eggplant on the grill directly over the heat and cook, with the lid down, for 20 or 30 minutes, turning every five minutes. The eggplant will puff up like a balloon during grilling.

3. Transfer the eggplant to a cutting board. Poke a hole or two in the eggplant skin with the tip of sharp knife; the eggplant will immediately deflate. Set aside to cool slightly.

4. When the eggplant is cool enough to handle, cut it in half, top to bottom, with a sharp knife. Using the edge of a spoon, scrape the soft flesh away from the skin. Put the flesh in a bowl. Add the tahini, garlic and mix. Drizzle with olive oil, dust with cumin, salt and pepper to taste, and top with the chopped parsley and toasted walnuts. Serve at room temperature.

A friend took a look at this painting and said "too bad you can't smell it." She was right: as wonderful as the fragrance of the cut fruit is, the scent of 'Meyer' lemon blossoms can only be described as ethereal.

'MEYER' LEMON SAUCE

I first ran across this recipe on Madalaine McDaniel's website called Lakeside Table. *The simplicity of it appealed to me but I also wondered if it was too simple to be true. As improbable as the recipe seems, believe me it's for real—smooth, elegant and very flavorful. Be advised that despite what I wrote back at the end of page 11, this is one of the few recipes that only works with 'Meyer' lemons, with their thin skins and minimal pith; if made with one of the standard sour lemon varieties, the sauce would be much too bitter and sharp. And another thing: a lot of home cooks, including myself, think when a recipe calls for straining anything, it's okay to skip that step, leaving the bits and pieces in the mix. This recipe is an instance where straining is absolutely necessary for the sauce to be a success. Do not skip this step. And do not mistake this for a dessert sauce. It is made to be used on top of fish or chicken and virtually any vegetable. Also good as a sauce for drizzling on pasta, such as the* Pasta with Tuna and Fried Lemons *on page 63. Madalaine advised leaving the seeds in; I took them out knowing that even though they were from a 'Meyer' lemon, they could still be bitter. To make sure you've removed all the seeds, hold the quarters up to a bright light; the seeds will show up as dark spots in the flesh of the lemon. After straining, makes a generous one-quarter cup, depending on the size of the lemon used.*

1 'Meyer' lemon, quartered, seeds removed
½ teaspoon salt
2 tablespoons water
¼ cup extra virgin olive oil

1. Put the quartered, de-seeded 'Meyer' lemon, salt, and water into a blender, peel and all. Process on high speed, slowly adding the olive oil in a thin stream. Add more water if necessary.

2. Strain sauce through a fine mesh sieve, pressing the mixture with the back of a spoon to get all the goodness into the sauce.

Note: Sauce can be made ahead of time and refrigerated in an air-tight container for seven days or frozen for up to three months.

This is one of my grandfather's ginger jars (see page 101), dating back to the 1920s. Yes, it really was filled with large chunks of ginger root, preserved in a thick sugar syrup. Pretty exotic when I was a kid.

EASY AÏOLI

I like authenticity and doing things the "right" way as much as the next cookbook writer, but there are times when what are now being called "hacks" (one of the examples Urban Dictionary *gives for "hack" is: "I didn't have time to do things properly, so I just hacked together something that worked). "Something that worked" is the operative phrase for this hack; it fills the bill for housemade aïoli just fine. With the possible exception of breakfast cereal, there's not much that isn't improved with the addition of a dollop of aïoli. Enjoy. Makes about three-quarters of a cup.*

2 – 3 cloves garlic, depending on your taste, finely grated, minced, or pressed
2 tablespoons 'Meyer' lemon juice (from 1 small lemon)
½ teaspoon Dijon mustard
¾ cup mayonnaise
Salt, to taste

1. Stir 5 finely grated garlic cloves, 1 tablespoon of the 'Meyer' lemon juice, and ½ teaspoon Dijon mustard together in a small bowl until combined. Let sit at room temperature for 15 minutes for the flavors to meld and mellow a bit.

2. Whisk in mayonnaise to the garlic/lemon mixture until smooth. Taste. Add additional kosher salt if needed and up to 1 tablespoon more lemon juice, depending on how "lemony" you like it.

About halfway through this painting I began to wonder what I had gotten myself into… I don't think I'll be painting any Japanese latticeware bowls in the near future.

AMY'S 'MEYER' SALSA

I love my friend Amy's cooking. Her 'Meyer' lemon chicken is featured on page 69. Her style is characterized by full-flavors and this recipe is no exception. Excellent on grilled fish or chicken. Makes about three-quarters of a cup.

1 'Meyer' lemon, very thinly sliced and diced
¼ cup shallot, minced
1½ tablespoons sherry vinegar
¼ cup finely-chopped curly parsley
2 tablespoons chives, finely chopped
⅓ cup extra virgin olive oil
Salt, to taste
Freshly ground pepper, to taste

Slice the lemons, including peel, as thinly as possible. Remove seeds. Chop the lemon slices into a small dice. Combine the diced lemons with the rest of the ingredients in a medium bowl. Stir to combine. Let stand 30 minutes for flavors to "marry." Will keep for several days, covered, in the refrigerator. If salsa seems a little dry after storing in the refrigerator, drizzle with a little more olive oil.

A cobalt blue and white checkered bowl is just about the perfect foil for the rich yellow of 'Meyer' lemons.

DON'S BLUE CHEESE DRESSING

This one goes back a ways—like a long ways. My friend Don, from U.C. Berkeley back in the early 70s introduced me to it, served on the classic wedge of crisp, cold iceberg lettuce. It was an excellent recipe back then and it still is today. I think it's one of the very few recipes that, over the span of some 50-plus years, I haven't felt the need to adapt or update for changing tastes. It's a consistent winner just as it is. For the record, I've made it with both vinegar and with juice from a standard sour lemon and neither are nearly as good as when it's made with 'Meyer' lemon juice. Adjust the amounts of the following ingredients according to your needs and tastes. If you like a thinner dressing, add a small amount of water—one teaspoonful at a time—thoroughly incorporating each addition until you reach the desired consistency.

Equal parts mayonnaise and sour cream
Fresh garlic, pressed
Juice of 'Meyer' lemon
Crumbled blue cheese, your choice, domestic or imported
Salt and freshly ground pepper, to taste

Put all the ingredients in a bowl and stir vigorously with a wooden spoon. Personally, I like it when some good-sized bits of blue cheese remain in the mix. Any leftovers can be stored in an airtight jar or other container in the refrigerator for up to a week.

Food professionals often describe the addition of fresh lemon juice and/or its zest as "brightening" a dish. It's as accurate a descriptor as any, made even more so when the lemon used is a 'Meyer.'

CAESAR SALAD DRESSING

Although there's some disagreement over the origins of the Caesar Salad, I'm siding with Caesar Cardini and his restaurant, Caesar's, in Tijuana, Mexico on the 4th of July, 1924. The salad is said to have been improvised with ingredients Caesar had on hand during the busy holiday weekend; it's been a perennial favorite for the hundred years since. For the record, the reason the restaurant was located in Tijuana was to avoid the laws regulating Prohibition in the States. Tijuana is only 17 miles from San Diego, which is why Caesar's had a nearly all-American clientele and why his patrons demanded the salad be made available in U.S. restaurants soon after he introduced it in Mexico. Makes about three-quarters of a cup.

6 anchovies in oil
2 egg yolks
3 garlic cloves
¼ cup 'Meyer' lemon juice
2 teaspoons Dijon mustard
½ cup extra virgin olive oil
½ cup Parmesan cheese, grated
Croutons

1. Caesar's dressing can be made using a food processor, a blender, an immersion blender, or even by hand, using a wire whisk. Whatever method you choose, the process is the same: combine the anchovy, egg yolks, garlic cloves, lemon juice, and Dijon mustard and mix until smooth and well-blended. Then add the olive oil in a steady stream; it should only take a minute or two for the sauce to thicken. Some folks like to add the Parmesan cheese directly to the dressing, others prefer adding it on top of the lettuce after it's been dressed. If after adding all of the oil, it seems too thick, add a teaspoon or two of water to thin it. Season with salt and pepper to taste.

2. Drizzle on top of crisp Romaine lettuce spears and scatter the croutons over all. It should be noted that it's perfectly acceptable to pick up the spears with your fingers, eating them as you would asparagus.

I was very complimented when a friend of mine—who happens to be a very fine artist—purchased this painting for his private collection.

'MEYER' LEMON CRAB LOUIE

This is one of my favorite go-to hot weather dishes. Beautiful to look at and delicious to eat. Served with warm, rustic French bread, this "salad" is substantial enough to be considered a main dish. If Dungeness crab is not available, bay shrimp is a tasty substitute. Serves four.

1½ pounds crab meat, preferably Dungeness
¼ cup 'Meyer' lemon juice
2 teaspoons grated 'Meyer' lemon zest
1 large head butter lettuce (reserve four of the biggest outside leaves)
Cherry tomatoes, cut in half
Cucumber slices
Green onions, sliced, both white and green parts
Red pepper, sliced into strips
Hearts of palm, chilled, cut into quarters, lengthwise
4 hard-boiled eggs, cut into quarters
8 'Meyer' lemon wedges

For dressing:
1 cup mayonnaise
¼ cup Sriracha or ketchup-based chili sauce
1 teaspoon grated 'Meyer' lemon zest

1. Mix the mayonnaise, Sriracha (or chili sauce) and lemon zest in a bowl. The amount of Sriracha sauce can be adjusted up or down, depending on your taste. Reserve in refrigerator.

2. In a large bowl, toss crab meat with lemon juice and zest. Keep in refrigerator until ready to use. Rinse and blot dry four, large, whole butter leaves and place one on each individual plate. Rough cut the remaining lettuce and divide equally on top of the four whole lettuce leaves. Arrange the tomatoes, cucumbers, hearts of palm, red pepper strips, lemon wedges and hard-boiled eggs on the perimeter of the lettuce. Add the dressed crab meat in the middle of the lettuce, in a neat pile. Scatter the green onions over all and pass the dressing. Good eating!

The best part of the day: something tasty on the grill, shadows lengthening, adult beverage close-at-hand and a 'Meyer' lemon bush laden with fruit—a beautiful part of the garden and an important component of many recipes.

GRILLED BASIL AND PROSCUITTO-WRAPPED PRAWNS

This appetizer is a triple threat if ever there was one: three simple ingredients that add up to much more than the sum of their parts. Serve these hot off the grill or at room temperature and be prepared to have them disappear faster than you thought possible. Because of their appeal, it's hard to say how many servings sixteen prawns makes. Note: *If you're lucky enough to have a garden, search out plants or seeds of 'Italian Large Leaf Basil' (sometimes sold as 'Genovese') for a ready supply of unusually large, flavorful basil leaves, perfect for wrapping.*

16 large raw prawns, peeled, tails on
16 large, whole basil leaves
16 very thin slices prosciutto
Freshly ground pepper to taste
Drizzle of olive oil
'Meyer' lemon wedges
Aïoli sauce (see page 45 for the recipe)

1. Preheat the grill with all the burners on high and the lid closed for ten minutes.

2. Rinse the peeled prawns in cold water. Blot dry on several thicknesses of paper towel.

3. Wrap each prawn with a whole basil leaf, followed by a slice of prosciutto; the natural stickiness of the prosciutto will hold the basil in place. No toothpick fastener needed. Drizzle wrapped prawns lightly with olive oil.

4. Turn all burners down to medium-high, place the wrapped shrimp on the grill and cook, with the lid open, for a total of approximately three minutes, 1½ minutes per side. Arrange prawns on serving platter, flanked by 'Meyer' lemon wedges and a bowl of aïoli. Seriously good.

My father brought this unusual platter back from Japan in the late 1960s, an era when many Japanese artists and craftspeople, as well as countless other creative types around the world, ventured beyond traditional subjects and styles. This large platter features stylized swirls of chrysanthemum flowers and foliage, painted blue!

'MEYER' LEMON FOCACCIA WITH LOX

Why hasn't someone come up with this before? It's seriously good, especially as the centerpiece for a sunny Sunday outdoor brunch and maybe, if you're feeling frisky, a Bloody Mary. Makes one 9- by 13-inch focaccia.

2 cups warm water, 105°F to 110°F
2 teaspoons yeast
2 teaspoons salt
4 cups bread flour
Zest of 4 'Meyer' lemons,
2 tablespoons capers, blotted dry between papertowels
½ cup extra virgin olive oil
Coarse salt for sprinking on top of focaccia, to taste
Sliced lox (store-bought)
'Meyer' lemon wedges

1. Preheat oven to 425°F. Put the yeast in a large mixing bowl and pour in the warm water. Add the salt and two cups of the flour and mix well.

2. Add the remaining two cups flour and mix well. Sprinkle half the lemon zest over the dough and all of the capers. Kneed the dough just enough to distribute the zest and capers through the dough. The dough will still be a bit sticky. Cover dough-filled bowl with a dish towel and let rise at warm room temperature until it doubles in size, between 40 minutes to an hour.

3. Add a liberal layer of olive oil to a 9- by 13-inch baking sheet and press the dough, using your fingers, into a rectangle that fills the baking sheet.

4. Using your fingers, add another liberal layer of olive oil to the top of the dough, leaving small olive oil filled depressions all across the surface. Sprinkle the remaining lemon zest on top, along with the coarse salt, to taste.

5. Bake for 18 to 25 minutes until lightly golden, turning the pan around every 10 minutes. Cut into manageable slices and top with lox and a squeeze of fresh 'Meyer' lemon juice for a memorable taste treat.

'Meyer' lemons are known for the ability to remain on the tree for relatively long periods time without much loss of quality. This is a welcome characteristic considering how big the typical 'Meyer' lemon crop is.

MARMALADE GLAZED SALMON

As I mentioned in the introduction to the marmalade recipe on page 31, the late olive oil maven, Nan McEvoy, suggested combining 'Meyer' lemon marmalade with soy sauce as glaze for salmon fillets or steaks. I'm not sure where I ran across Nan's idea, but it sure sounded like a good one. A couple of cautions: Don't allow the salmon to sit too long coated in the soy/marmalade mixture—30 minutes max—any longer and the flavors will become too strong and the salmon will start to "cure." Because of the amount of sugar in the marmalade, you'll need to watch the cooking temperature and the cooking time carefully. If you pan-sear the salmon in a non-stick pan that's been thoroughly preheated over low-medium heat, you'll have much more control over the degree of doneness than if you try to broil or grill it. Remember, the goal is to brown the salmon, not burn the marinade.

Salmon fillets or steaks, 6 to 8-ounces for each diner
For the marinade/glaze for each fillet or steak, mix together:
1 tablespoon 'Meyer' lemon marmalade (or other citrus marmalade)
1 tablespoon soy sauce
1 tablespoon 'Meyer' lemon juice
Flavorless oil for adding to the pan before adding the salmon

1. Preheat non-stick skillet over low-medium heat for at least 5 minutes. Just before adding the salmon fillets or steaks, add a thin layer of vegetable oil and swirl around to evenly coat the pan. If the fillets have skin, place them skin side down to start.

2. The degree of doneness is a matter of personal preference but, generally speaking, you're looking at approximately 3 to 4 minutes per side to keep everyone happy. The salmon is done when it turns opaque and flakes easily with a twist of a fork.

3. Serve hot out of the pan with wedges of fresh 'Meyer' lemons. Delicious with rice and steamed baby bok choy, doused with rice vinegar.

Some flavors just go together, like lemons and any kind of seafood. It's hard to say exactly what makes the pairing so complementary, but it is very apparent in the recipe presented at right.

CONFIT OF TUNA

Inspired by a recipe that originally appeared in The New York Times, *this dish is the real deal. Absolutely delicious as part of an antipasto platter, tossed with pasta (see page 63), or in a Salade Niçoise. In the ten years since writing the first edition of this book, this recipe has been in regular rotation at my house.*

1 pound tuna (albacore or yellowfin), fresh or thawed frozen, 1-inch-thick, cut into 1-inch cubes
1 teaspoon salt
½ teaspoon red pepper flakes
2 tablespoons thinly-sliced garlic
Freshly ground black pepper, to taste
1 bay leaf
Zest and juice of one-half 'Meyer' lemon
1 cup olive oil, plus more if necessary

1. Trim any skin, bones or dark blood spots from the tuna and discard. Place the cubes of tuna in a 1-quart saucepan (if the pan is too big, you'll use too much olive oil—the cubes should fit snugly in the pan). Add the salt, red pepper flakes, garlic and black pepper and stir gently to distribute seasonings evenly. Add the bay leaf and lemon zest and lemon juice and pour enough olive oil to just barely cover the fish. It will be about 1 cup, though you may need a little more for topping off.

2. Place the saucepan over low heat; the oil may get hot enough that a few bubbles rise from the bottom, but it should not actually simmer. Cook for about 15 minutes until the cubes have changed color, indicating they are just cooked.

3. Let the tuna cool to warm room temperature in the oil before transferring to a storage container. If you're going to use the tuna the same day, refrigeration is not necessary. If refrigerated, the tuna will keep, tightly sealed, for at least a week, but not more than ten days. Warm to room temperature before using. Just excellent!

An homage to the surrealistic Belgian painter, René Magritte. Among his many well-known images from the first half of the 20th century, were things like hats or apples whimsically floating in midair, defying gravity and making for amusing, memorable paintings.

PASTA WITH TUNA, GREEN OLIVES AND FRIED LEMONS

A decade or so ago, this dish started out as a New York Times *recipe for Pasta With Fried Lemons and Chile Flakes. Over the years it morphed into the recipe presented here—a keeper if I do say so myself. If you keep a few cans of good quality tuna packed in oil in your pantry—or just happen to have Confit of Tuna (previous recipe, page 61) made and in your refrigerator—you should be able to make this satisfying dish from ingredients you have on hand. As a rule, Italian cooks do not add cheese to any pasta containing seafood. You'll find the toasted panko breadcrumbs are an excellent alternative. Feeds four generously.*

1 pound long, thin pasta, such as bucatini, spaghetti, or linguine
1½ 'Meyer' lemons
4 tablespoons extra virgin olive oil, more for drizzling (optional)
4 large cloves garlic, thinly sliced
4 scallions, thinly sliced, white and green parts separated
6 to 10 anchovies, chopped
¾ cup pitted green olives, sliced in half, lengthwise
½ cup chopped parsley, plus more for serving (optional)
1 cup dry white wine
3 cans (about 4-ounces each) tuna in oil, drained and chunked
½ cup panko breadcrumbs
Red-pepper flakes, for serving
'Meyer' lemon wedges, for serving

1. Heat 1 tablespoon olive oil in a large skillet over medium heat. Trim the tops and bottoms off the lemons and cut lengthwise into quarters; remove seeds. Thinly slice the quarters crosswise into triangles. In the same skillet, heat an additional 1 tablespoon of olive oil over medium-high heat. Add the lemon triangles and cook until the edges of the lemons start to brown, 3 to 5 minutes. Transfer to a plate.

2. Add panko to the same skillet. Stir constantly until golden brown (about 3-5 minutes). Transfer panko to a separate paper towel lined plate.

continued on page 96

A bounty of 'Meyer' lemons in a wooden bowl, ready for juicing and then freezing in ice cube trays. Once the cubes are completely frozen, remove them from the trays and store in zippered plastic bags until needed.

CLAM FETTUCINE

I don't know about you, but I feel better knowing I've got all the ingredients for a few different dishes that I can make without leaving the house—eating out of the pantry, you know? I've been making this dish forever and it still satisfies. Somewhere along the way I discovered that canned whole baby clams are far superior to those small cans of chopped clams. If you're in the mood for a dish a little more soupy, keep a couple of bottles of clam juice in your pantry along with the other ingredients; add as much as desired. The following recipe is for two servings; it can be easily scaled up to serve more diners.

4 tablespoons extra virgin olive oil
¼ cup panko breadcrumbs
2-3 large garlic cloves, thinly sliced
2 anchovy fillets
1 10-ounce can of whole baby clams
1 'Meyer' lemon, both zest and juice
½ cup dry white wine or dry vermouth
6 ounces linguine or spaghetti (a generous, main course serving)
¼ teaspoon chile flakes, more to taste
Black pepper, to taste
¼ cup celery leaves, chopped (if they're on hand)
¼ cup parsley, chopped
½ cup reserved pasta water (probably won't need it all)

1. In a large skillet, heat 1 tablespoon of the olive oil over medium-high heat. Add the panko and cook until toasted, 3 to 4 minutes. Transfer to paper towel lined plate. Add more olive oil if needed; add the garlic and anchovies and cook until the garlic is golden and the anchovies dissolve (about 3 minutes). Transfer to another plate.

2. Bring a large pot of salted water to a boil. Add the pasta to the boiling water; cook until just al dente. Drain, reserving ½ cup of the pasta cooking water.

continued on page 96

It seems that several people misunderstood this painting, thinking I had stabbed the lemon. Not so: my pocketknife is stuck into the cutting board, not *the lemon.*

SHRIMP TACOS

These appear regularly around here, simply because they're so darned good. As far as a complementary combination of flavors and textures go, in my opinion these tacos are right near the top of the list. Heat the corn tortillas any way you want, but in the interest of simplicity, I've taken to heating a couple of tortillas at a time in the toaster oven set on "Toast" to the point where they are thoroughly heated but still bendable. And in the interest of space, I am not going to try and explain the differences between shrimp and prawns, other than to say that they can be used interchangably and they both benefit from very brief cooking.

Large shrimp (20 to 25 to the pound), two per taco
Vegetable oil
Chile-Lime seasoning (such as Tajin)
Fresh cabbage, coarsely shredded
Fresh cilantro, roughly chopped
Avocado, one generous slice per taco
'Meyer' lemon
Secret Sauce (your favorite fresh salsa mixed with mayonnaise, about half-and-half)
Your favorite bottled hot sauce

1. Sprinkle shrimp/prawns with Chili-Lime seasoning and sauté quickly over medium-high heat in a little vegetable oil until they just turn pink and curl into a C-shape; if they form a tight O-shape, the shrimp/prawns will be over-cooked.

2. Place a generous layer of cabbage and cilantro on warmed tortilla

3. Add avocado slice and a couple of prawns on top of cabbage/cilantro mixture. Squeeze 'Meyer' lemon over all ingredients.

4. Drizzle Secret Sauce over the top, along with as much of your favorite hot sauce as you want.

5. Ready for a major taste treat? Best eaten leaning over the sink.

A French drying cloth, with its rich blue stripe, seemed like the perfect contrasting partner for this pair of 'Meyer' lemons, all reflected in the silver julep cup.

AMY'S ROAST 'MEYER' CHICKEN

Amy is a good friend of mine and one of the best cooks I know. Her dishes all have a distinctive California flare and this 'Meyer' lemon chicken is no exception. Amy roasts hers in the oven; you'll find instructions for oven roasting on page 97. Because a whole roast chicken is a dramatic and delicious thing to cook outside, most readers will want to use their gas grill, instructions for which you'll find below. I prefer the Old School method of cooking it on my trusty Weber charcoal grill, using the indirect method, with the coals on one side of the grate and the chicken on the other side of the grill, lid on, vent holes completely open, positioned over the chicken. Which ever method you choose, I can just about guarantee that you're in store for a first-class meal. Serves four to six.

1 whole chicken, 3½ to 4 pounds
2 'Meyer' lemons, cut in half for juicing
Salt and freshly ground black pepper, to taste (be generous)
2 large sprigs fresh rosemary
1 large head garlic, individual cloves smashed and peeled
2 tablespoons butter, softened

1. Preheat the grill with all the burners on high for ten minutes and the lid down.

2. Fold the wing tips under the back of the chicken. Put one sprig of rosemary in the middle of a roasting pan not much larger than the chicken. Place the chicken on top of the rosemary; place the other rosemary sprig inside the cavity. Juice the lemons and pour over the chicken, both inside and out. Break the garlic head into cloves, smash them with the side of a broad knife and discard peels; and add a few to the cavity and the rest to the pan around the chicken. Rub the softened butter across the breasts and tops of drumsticks. Generously salt and pepper the chicken inside and out.

3. Once the grill is hot, turn off the center burner and turn the other burners to medium. With the chicken breast side up in the roasting pan, place it over the center burner and close the lid. Cook until the juices run clear

continued on page 96

The best thing about making your own lemonade—besides how fresh it tastes—is the control you have in making it as sweet (or not) as you want.

BEST-EVER CHICKEN THIGHS

Perfectly delicious and wonderfully easy! If you thought you knew everything there was to know about cooking chicken, think again. This method, originally set forth by Paul Bertolli in his book Cooking by Hand, *was then modified by Melissa Hamilton and Christopher Hirsheimer of Canal House fame. Bertolli called the cooking method "bottom-up cooking." (He should receive an award for unleashing it on the world). Essentially you pan fry chicken thighs over medium-low heat for approximately 20 minutes per side, flipping once only. I further modified it because I wanted a simple pan sauce to serve with the chicken. As far as I'm concerned, this is about as good as food gets. If you have a seasoned cast iron pan, just the right size to hold the thighs, this would be the time to use it. Serves four.*

4 large chicken thighs, skin on, bone in
Salt and freshly ground pepper, to taste
Rind from ¼ of a preserved lemon (see recipe, page 29 or store-bought), lightly rinsed and diced
⅓ cup dry vermouth or dry white wine
⅓ cup chicken broth
1 teaspoon flour
1 tablespoon butter
'Meyer' lemon wedges and chopped fresh parsley, for garnish

1. Preheat pan over medium heat. Salt and pepper the thighs to your taste. Reduce heat to medium-low and place chicken, skin side down, for 20 minutes. Resist the temptation to fuss with them in any way. Do not cover pan. Turn thighs over and cook for an additional 20 minutes—again, no pushing, pulling, poking, or prodding!

2. Place cooked chicken on a platter and loosely tent with foil. Add the minced preserved lemon peel to the skillet. Increase heat to medium and add flour to the pan juices; whisk to mix. Add the wine and broth and continue to whisk until it thickens slightly. Whisk in butter and pour on top of chicken thighs. Garnish with chopped parsley and lemon wedges.

'Meyer' lemon plants are so prolific that the home gardener has to watch that they don't set too many fruits. The laden branches may become so heavy they are susceptible to breakage—like this one from my own garden. I should have been more diligent thinning the crop back in the fall when the lemons were small.

'MEYER' LEMON TURKEY PICCATA

I discovered using turkey tenders in this dish by accident—a happy accident as they are better, I think, than the more traditional veal scallops—not to mention a fraction of the cost. Turkey tenderloins are the long, tender strips of white meat hidden under the turkey breast. Serves four generously.

2 large 'Meyer' lemons
2 boneless, skinless turkey tenderloins, sliced into ⅜-inch thick slices
Salt, to taste
Freshly ground black pepper, to taste
¼ cup flour in a shaker or sieve
4 tablespoons olive oil
1 small shallot, minced (about 2 tablespoons)
½ cup chicken broth
½ cup dry vermouth
2 tablespoons capers, drained
3 tablespoons unsalted butter, softened
2 tablespoons fresh parsley, minced

1. Slice half of one lemon into ⅛-inch slices. Juice the remaining 1½ lemons; you should have about ¼ cup. Set aside.

2. Season both sides of the turkey tender slices with salt and pepper. Dust tenders with flour on all sides.

3.Heat two tablespoons of olive oil in a large, heavy-bottomed skillet over medium-high heat. Sauté the turkey slices approximately one minute per side. Add the minced shallot and cook, stirring, for another minute. Add the chicken broth, dry vermouth and lemon slices. Allow to cook until lemon slices are softened.

4. Add the capers and lemon juice; reduce slightly to concentrate flavors. Remove pan from heat and swirl in the butter until it melts and thickens the sauce. Sprinkle with parsley and serve immediately over a bed of steamed rice, orzo pasta, or couscous.

As traditionally appealing as lemons are combined with cobalt blue, some times it's good to experiment with other combinations—like this intense turquoise tile. The colors almost vibrate, don't they?

'MEYER' LEMON POSSET

This super simple, elegant dessert suffers, like clafoutis and syllabub—with a terrible name. People don't know how to pronounce any of them, let alone know what they are. For the record, posset is pronounced as it is spelled, like the English word "posit." If you're unfamiliar with posset, it's so easy and delicious, there's no reason not to give it a try. Serves four.

1 cup heavy cream
⅓ cup sugar
Pinch of salt
¼ cup 'Meyer' lemon juice (probably two lemons)
Zest of one 'Meyer' lemon and a mint leaf for garnish, if desired

1. Combine cream, sugar, and salt in a small saucepan; stir to combine. Heat over medium-low heat. Watch the mixture carefully and remove from the heat just as the mixture just comes to a boil. Let the mixture cool, stirring occasionally, about 15 or 20 minutes.

2. While mixture is cooling, zest one of the lemons for use as a garnish. Squeeze the lemons (including the one you used for zest) until you have ¼ cup juice. Lightly whisk the lemon juice into the cool cream mixture. It will start to thicken almost immediately. Pour into four of your most distinctive small glasses or demitasse cups. This is a rich dessert so you don't want to serve too much. Place in refrigerator to set for a least four hours. Garnish with the lemon zest or a mint leaf, or both. Serve with a couple of *Langues de Chat* or other crunchy cookie.

Standard, widely available sour lemons are the true yellow ones pictured at top right. 'Meyer' lemons are usually slightly smaller and rounder, more orangey-yellow in color and noticeably less sour and more perfumed, shown at the bottom left. They are also very juicy.

'MEYER' LEMON CURD

Count me among the home cooks who find making lemon curd the traditional way—using a double boiler—unnecessarily demanding and time-consuming. I much prefer making it over direct heat, which only takes about 10 minutes, from start to finish. Yes, it requires careful attention while whisking it over the heat, but it's completely do-able. Don't worry, you'll do fine. Note: *This is one of those procedures where the equipment is as important as the ingredients. Use a medium-size, heavy-bottomed, non-reactive pan—stainless steel or enamel- or ceramic-lined. Makes 1½ cups.*

⅓ to ½ cup granulated sugar, depending on your sweet tooth
Zest of 3 'Meyer' lemons; avoid the white pith, which can be bitter
½ cup 'Meyer' lemon juice, seeds removed
2 large eggs, plus 2 yolks
Pinch of salt (even if using salted butter)
6 tablespoons butter, in small pieces (cold is okay)

1. Set a fine mesh sieve over a bowl; slice the butter into pats. Set both aside.

2. Pour the sugar into a pan then zest the lemons over it. Using your fingers, massage the zest and sugar together; this produces the maximum 'Meyer' lemon flavor.

3. Add lemon juice (with seeds removed) to sugar and zest mixture. Whisk to combine.

4. In a separate bowl, beat the eggs with a pinch of salt, using a fork.

5. Pour the eggs into the pot with the zest, sugar, and lemon juice and whisk until everything is well-combined.

6. Set the pan over medium heat. Whisk constantly at a steady pace. The mixture will get foamy and then start to thicken. Once it starts to thicken it thickens rapidly. Whisk vigorously and do not let boil. The curd is done when it

continued on page 97

My favorite cutting board from Thailand. Made of super hard, dense tamarind wood, this round cutting board also has a handy handle, making it easy to take the whole thing over to a pot rather than bringing the pot to the cutting board.

'MEYER' LEMON MESS

This is one of those instances where you come up with an idea on your own, only to find out it's already been in existence for a very long time. A few years back I came up with this totally original (or so I thought) dessert to serve at the end of a Christmas dinner. There was unanimous agreement around the table that it was a keeper and I've been making it ever since. Then, a year or so ago, I came across a reference for an English dessert with the unlikely name of "Eton Mess." The dessert was first mentioned in historian Arthur Beavan's 1896 book titled Marlborough House and Its Occupants. *In a chapter detailing "notable balls, fêtes, and garden parties" at the royal residence, he notes that "Eton Mess aux Fraises," or Eton Mess with Strawberries, was served at an 1893 garden party that Queen Victoria attended. Many, however, attribute the creation of the dessert to Eton College, the posh boys' school in Windsor, England. There are iterations of Eton Mess throughout Britain, even a version with bananas—called Lancing Mess—served at Lancing College in Sussex. So much for originality.*

I make this concoction with homemade 'Meyer' lemon curd, which is wonderful. For the record, commercially made 'Meyer' lemon curd is available, but is somewhat hard to find. If you want to substitute regular lemon curd, there's no shame in doing so and if you use store-bought meringue cookies, you have an exceptional no-cook dessert.

How you assemble the dessert is entirely up to you, as there really isn't a recipe. Some smush everything—the whipped cream, meringues, fruit and ice cream—together in a large bowl, then spoon it into individual bowls to serve. Others carefully layer the components to create a kind of free-form parfait. When I came up with the idea, I had no idea it was a dessert with a history, served to no less than Queen Victoria. It's definitely stood the test of time—and for good reason!

Lemon curd, made with 'Meyer' lemons (see recipe page 77)
Whipped cream, lightly sweetened
Best quality vanilla ice cream
Meringue cookies, roughly crumbled

Combine any way you like, in any proportion, and it will be delicious, guaranteed.

I'm always on the lookout for interesting plates and platters that might complement 'Meyer' lemons. This one, with its unusual black-and-white decoration, really fit the bill.

'MEYER' LEMON SHAKER PIE

From its humble beginnings, the Shaker Lemon Pie has passed into something approaching cult status. Three things about this recipe: 1) It's wonderful, 2) it's not mine—it belongs to the remarkable Deb Perelman of the equally remarkable website www.smittenkitchen.com *and 3) kids will probably hate it and adults will probably love it. Let's just say it's intense.*

2 large 'Meyer' lemons, zested first and then very thinly sliced
2 cups granulated sugar
¼ teaspoon salt
4 eggs, lightly beaten
4 tablespons butter, melted
3 tablespoons all-purpose flour
1 egg white
Coarse sugar, for sprinkling
Dough for one double-crust pie

1. Thoroughly wash and dry lemons. Finely grate lemon zest into a bowl. Using a mandoline, slice lemons as paper thin as you can possibly get them; remove and discard seeds. Add slices to zest and toss with sugar and salt. Cover and set aside at room temperature for 24 hours.

2. Preheat the oven to 425°F. Roll out half the dough ⅛-inch thick on a lightly-floured surface, fit it into a 9-inch pie plate, and trim the edge, leaving a ½-inch overhang.

3. Mix the macerated lemon-sugar mixture with the four eggs, melted butter and flour until combined well. Pour into prepared pie shell.

4. Roll out the remaining dough into a 12-inch round on a lightly-floured surface, drape it over the filling, and trim it, leaving a 1-inch overhang. Fold the overhang under the bottom crust, pressing the edge to seal it, and crimp the edge. Beat one egg white until frothy and brush over pie crust, then sprinkle with coarse sugar.

continued on page 98

Those new to 'Meyer' lemons are surprised at how heavy individual fruits are—indicative of how much juice they contain.

'MEYER' LEMON AMOR POLENTA

I'm not sure where this old-fashioned recipe came from, only that it is a traditional tea cake from northern Italy. The cake itself became a favorite the first time I tried it, decades ago, in its hometown of Varese. I love it just as it is, especially with a cup of strong coffee (or tea). For the record, amor polenta translates, fittingly, into English as "Polenta Love."

⅔ cup butter, softened, plus more for preparing pan
2 cups powdered sugar, plus more for dusting finished cake
Pinch of salt
1 tablespoon 'Meyer' lemon zest
1 teaspoon vanilla
2 eggs plus 1 egg yolk
1 teaspoon baking powder
1¼ cups flour
⅓ cup cornmeal, plus more for dusting pan

1. Preheat oven to 350°F. Using an electric mixer, cream the butter and powdered sugar in a large bowl. Add the salt, lemon zest, vanilla, eggs and extra egg yolk to the creamed butter and sugar mixture and mix thoroughly.

3. Add the flour, cornmeal, and baking powder to the butter-sugar-egg mixture; mix until thoroughly incorporated. Pour batter into a buttered saddle pan* dusted with cornmeal. Bake for 40 to 50 minutes, until a skewer or toothpick inserted in the cake comes out clean. Allow cake to cool. Place, curved side up, on plate; dust with powdered sugar.

* *"And what exactly is a saddle pan?"* you might ask. Right after I wrote "saddle pan" I realized I didn't really know what that meant, only that I had one and it only gets used when I make amor polenta. The pan has a long, half-round shape (when viewed from the end of the pan) and is deeply ridged. The ridges make it easy to slice the cake into uniform slices and is, simply, the traditional pan for making this cake. Sometimes, when it comes to traditions, it doesn't pay to dig too deeply into why things are the way they are. They just are. Suffice it to say if you don't have saddle pan, a loaf pan works fine.

I'll tell you one thing—after doing the paintings for this book, I definitely had a new-found appeciation for the craftspeople who apply the designs and patterns on porcelain.

‘MEYER’ LEMON PUDDING CAKE

I’m a sucker for pudding cakes and this one’s unique smooth, somewhat wiggly texture is particularly good, almost like mochi (a special Japanese rice cake). It originally appeared on the Epicurious website many years ago. Over time, it’s undergone a few tweaks which, I think, have made a very good thing even better. The fresh berries are a wonderful complement.

1½ cups buttermilk
1 cup granulated sugar, divided in half
4 large eggs, separated
⅓ cup ‘Meyer’ lemon juice
1 tablespoon ‘Meyer’ lemon zest
¼ cup all-purpose flour
¼ cup butter, melted
⅛ teaspoon salt
Any fresh berries

1. Preheat the oven to 350°F. Butter 8- by 8-inch glass baking dish. Blend buttermilk, ½ cup sugar, egg yolks, lemon juice and zest, flour, butter, and salt in a blender until smooth. Transfer the buttermilk mixture to a medium bowl. Using an electric mixer, beat egg whites in a separate large bowl until soft peaks form. Gradually add remaining sugar and beat until stiff but not dry. Gently fold the beaten egg whites into the buttermilk mixture, one-third at a time. Batter will be runny.

2. Pour batter into prepared dish. Place dish in a larger roasting pan. Pour enough hot water into the roasting pan to come halfway up the sides of the baking dish. Bake until entire top is evenly browned and cake moves very slightly in the center but feels springy to the touch, about 45 minutes.

3. Remove cake from water bath and allow to cool on a rack. Refrigerate until cold, at least three hours and up to six hours. Spoon pudding cake out into shallow bowls and top with fresh berries of your choice.

Finally found the painting I was looking for: The Last One!

1-2-3-4 CAKE WITH 'MEYER' LEMON CURD FILLING

For as popular as this cake once was, particularly in the South, it's surprising how few people have heard of it, let alone made one. Talk about old-fashioned goodness! It's a classic birthday cake, open to all sorts of variations, from strawberry jam filling to sliced bananas and whipped cream. That said, over many years, our household has settled on 'Meyer' lemon curd filling between the layers, combined with buttercream frosting on the outside and top. With a scoop of good vanilla ice cream, it'll be a happy birthday, indeed. See page 98 for Buttercream Frosting recipe.

1 cup butter
2 cups sugar
4 eggs
3 cups cake flour
3 teaspoons baking powder
½ teaspoon baking soda
1 teaspoon salt
1¼ buttermilk
1½ teaspoons vanilla

1. Make 'Meyer' Lemon Curd (page 77) and allow to completely cool.

2. Preheat oven to 350°F. Prepare three 8- or 9-inch cake pans with butter or baking spray and flour.

3. Using a stand mixer, cream the butter and sugar until fluffy, 3 or 4 minutes. Add whole eggs to butter and sugar mixture, one at a time, and mix well after each addition. Beat in vanilla.

4. Turn off mixer. In a large bowl, sift together flour, baking powder, baking soda and salt. With the mixer on low, add the flour mixture to the butter mixture, a cup at a time, alternating with buttermilk. When smooth, divide the batter between the three cake pans. Bake in a 350°F oven and start testing for doneness at 35 minutes until a wooden

continued on page 98

A PRIMER ON THE CARE, FEEDING & TRAINING OF 'MEYER' LEMONS

The information on the following eight pages is adapted from the website of *Four Winds Growers*—a family-owned nursery specializing primarily in citrus. They have been in the business selling plants to home gardeners since 1948 and they, arguably, know as much as anyone about the subject. The information is divided between growing 'Meyer' lemons outdoors in the landscape, outdoors in containers, and growing indoors.

Growing Outdoors in the Landscape

Generally speaking, the citrus family is a group of willing-to-grow species, as long as the climatic conditions where they are planted fall in an acceptable range. Optimum results, however, especially in terms of fruit quality, require matching the climate requirements of the type of citrus you're growing to the conditions in your garden more closely. Unlike some other types of citrus, 'Meyer' lemons do not require a great deal of summer heat to ripen, preferring a moderate climate (ideal temperatures between 50–80°F). And they are more cold-hardy than true lemons, being able to withstand temperatures down to 20°F. That said, to avoid damage, cover 'Meyer' lemon plants with some type of frost protection when temperatures are forecast to fall below 40°F.

Quick 'Meyer' Facts

- *'Meyer' lemons are self-fertile, meaning single plants don't require a pollinizer to produce fruit.*

- *The word "Improved" denotes the 'Meyer' lemon is a virus-free strain developed to replace plants which carried the citrus triteza virus. Virtually all 'Meyer' lemons today are of the 'Improved' variety, whether it's part of its name or not.*

- *'Meyer' lemon plants bloom almost continuously, often bearing white fragrant flowers, small green immature fruit, and mature, golden-yellow ripe fruit, all at the same time.*

Location. 'Meyer' lemon plants require 6 to 8 hours of full sun daily. If you live in a cool climate, make the most of what sun and warmth you have by planting in a south-facing location or by training the plant as an espalier (see illustration page 92). Just keep in mind that 'Meyer' lemons do not require high temperatures to produce flavorful fruit and that too much heat can actually reduce fruit set.

Planting. Early spring through early summer is an ideal time to plant 'Meyer' lemons directly in the ground. Dig a hole twice as wide as the container it came in from the nursery, but no deeper. Remove the plant from the pot and place in the hole, preferably on undisturbed soil, which is not likely to settle, causing the lemon to sink. The top of the rootball should be slightly above the native soil level. Use a quality potting soil mixed with about a one-third addition of commerically available compost. Backfill the hole with this mixture and tamp it down to get rid of air pockets. Water deeply after planting.

Water. Citrus trees need regular watering during the non-rainy months. On the other hand, they do not tolerate constantly wet soil, so it's best to allow the soil to dry out somewhat between waterings; don't water already wet soil. Check your soil moisture level regularly by sticking your finger up

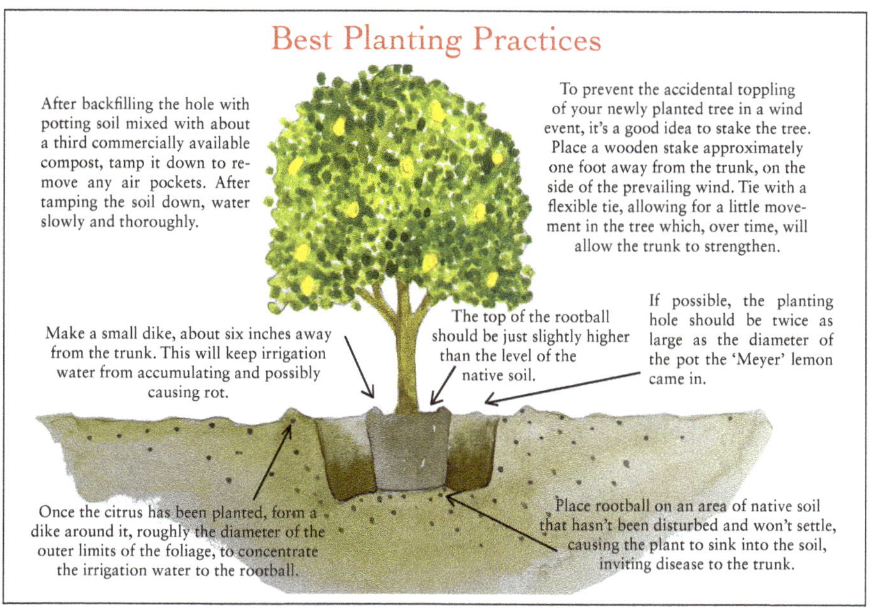

to the second knuckle into the soil to see if it is dry. A deep watering once a week is a safe place to start but, of course, every climate and your local weather conditions will vary, influencing the frequency of your watering practices. If your tree's foliage is wilting, you're not watering frequently enough. Forming a dike to hold the irrigation water is a good practice around any citrus plant—just make sure to make it about as wide as the spread of the foliage. It's also a good idea to include an additional small dike, six inches or so from the trunk, to keep the irrigation water from settling around it, potentially causing problems with rot. When you water, water thoroughly, to a depth of three feet or more.

Feeding. Feed the 'Meyer' lemon with a balanced fertilizer (one specially formulated for citrus, if available) monthly during the spring and summer and early fall months. These are considered the growing months. Apply it according to the manufacturer's instructions. Remember: A weaker dilution of fertilizer is better than too much or too strong a dose. And if any of your citrus are showing signs of chlorosis (yellowing leaves in one form or another), be sure and use a specially formulated product containing chelated iron, zinc, and manganese. Read and follow all label instructions.

Pruning. In the early spring, prune the tree to maintain a desirable shape and remove dead or diseased branches. Remember that vertical branches focus on vegetative growth while horizontal or semi-horizontal branches are devoted to fruiting.

Pests and diseases. Small infestations are much easier to control than larger ones, so it's a good idea keep your eye out for common citrus pests like aphids, scale insects, and whiteflies and diseases like sooty mold. If you find any infestations, treat your tree with the least toxic options first. There are many effective horticultural oils and insecticidal soaps available at nurseries and garden centers. For the best results, read and follow all label instructions carefully.

Varieties & Sizes

'Meyer' lemons are available as plants which mature to three different sizes, determined by the "Three Ways to Keep a 'Meyer' Lemon Small," discussed below. It pays to give some thought to which size is best-suited to your garden and the space available. The plant may be small when you plant it, but it will grow relatively quickly to its mature size and you don't want it to outgrow its location in your garden.

Dwarf: Grafted onto a dwarfing rootstock, often the one known as 'Flying Dragon,' dwarf plants are ideal for pots, typically staying around 4 to 6 feet tall, but can be kept even smaller with pruning.

Semi-Dwarf: The most popular choice, growing 8 to 12 feet tall in the ground or 6 to 8 feet in pots, optimum sizes for most home gardeners.

Standard/Full Size: These grow larger but 'Meyer' lemons are naturally smaller than most other citrus varieties, reaching a maximum height of up to 12 to 15 feet; some gardeners prune standard-sized trees regularly to stay even smaller.

Three Ways to Keep a 'Meyer' Lemon Small

The three main factors in determining the size of your plant are what rootstock your 'Meyer' lemon is grafted onto, whether it's being grown in a container or directly in the landscape, and how it's being pruned.

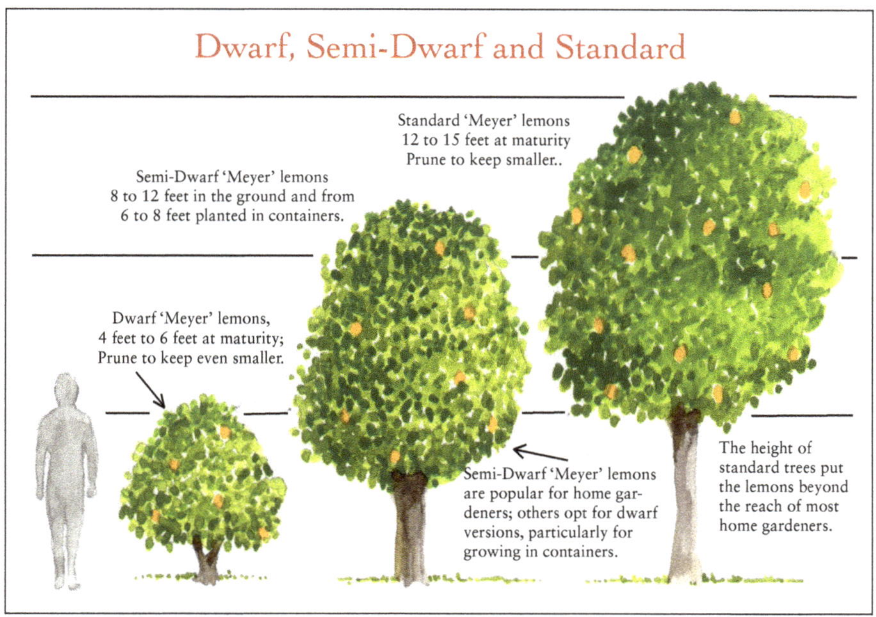

Rootstock: Grafting a 'Meyer' lemon plant onto a dwarfing rootstock, such as 'Flying Dragon,' is the primary factor determining the ultimate size of the plant. The use of 'Flying Dragon' also adds considerable cold tolerance to the plants, allowing them to be grown in cooler climates. Be sure and keep the suckers that sprout from below the graft union pruned, as these will have the characteristics of 'Flying Dragon' rootstock, not the desired tree.

Espaliered Citrus

The history of training citrus on a flat plane (called "espaliering") dates back to ancient Egypt and Rome. It started as a practical way to to maximize fruit production in small, walled gardens and as a way to make the most of reflected warmth from the typically stone walls, protecting citrus planted in marginal, cold winter climates. As good as espaliers were for solving practical problems, over the centuries monastic gardeners began to employ the practice of espaliering for its beauty, using more and more intricate and attractive patterns. 'Meyer' lemons are particularly well-suited to training as espaliers and a real focal point in the winter garden when they display their bright golden yellow ripe fruit. Remember when you're training the branches, that vertical ones produce the least fruit and horizontal ones produce the most.

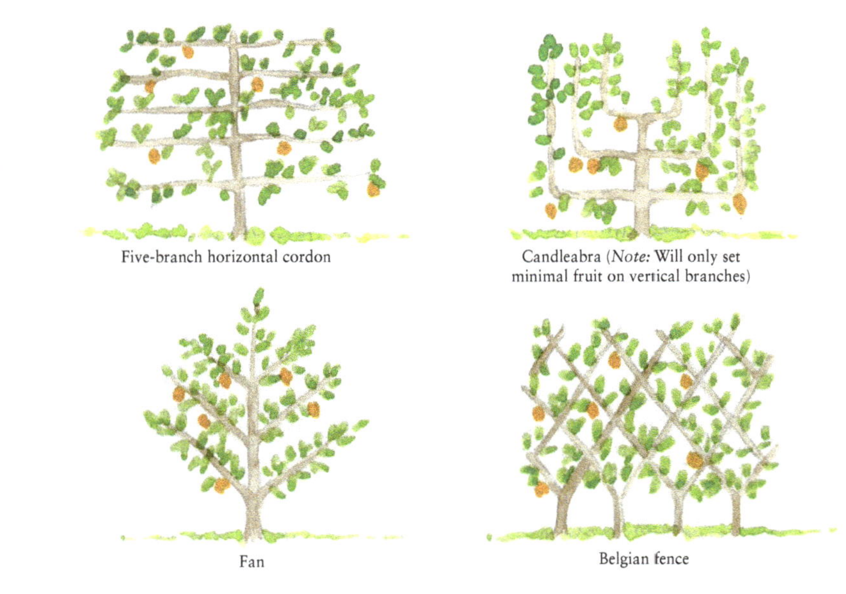

Five-branch horizontal cordon

Candleabra (*Note:* Will only set minimal fruit on vertical branches)

Fan

Belgian fence

Container Growing: Expect any citrus planted in a container to be smaller in stature than the same variety, grafted onto the same rootstock, than if it were planted in the ground. Simply put, planting in pots naturally restricts plant size, regardless of the rootstock it's grown on.

Pruning: All 'Meyer' lemons benefit from pruning, but it's also a very practical and immediate way of controlling the size and shape of your 'Meyer' lemon plant. Most home gardeners desire trees whose fruit can be harvested without the aid of a ladder and prune with that end in mind.

Growing in Containers

Overall, citrus trees are naturally well-suited for container growing, especially 'Meyer' lemons, which are naturally small in stature compared to other citrus. Growing in containers allows gardeners to overcome poor native soils or limited space in a landscape. People enjoy their trees in decorative pots on patios and apartment balconies. With judicious pruning, any citrus can be kept at a manageable size.

Drainage. When growing any citrus in containers, be sure there are sufficient holes to provide excellent drainage. Drilling extra holes is an easy way to improve drainage with wood or plastic containers. And don't start with a too-large pot that makes the moisture level of the soil hard to control. Too much extra soil tends to stay wet for too long, causing "root rot" or "wet feet." Be sure the pot never sits in standing drainage water. If you're using a saucer under the pot, add a layer of small river rocks to it to keep the container sitting above the drainage water.

Soil. Finding the perfect high porosity soil mix can be hard to find. Best bet is to look for a commercially available mix especially formulated for citrus or citrus and cactus. To keep container-grown citrus healthy over the long haul, it's a good idea to add about one-third commercially available compost to the mix, by proportion. This should provide the right balance of drainage, water retention, and the aeration your tree will need to flourish. Using native soil/dirt from your yard is not recommended. The use of a layer of gravel at the bottom of the pot can also negatively impact drainage over time, but is a good idea for filling saucers, holding the bottom of the pot above the drainage water that usually accumulates there, thereby avoiding problems associated with soil that remains too wet over long periods of time.

For citrus growing indoors or out, favor potting soils labeled for outdoor use as opposed to mixes made for indoor growing. Indoor mixes often contain chemical wetting agents, causing tree roots to remain too wet after watering, and fertilizers already in the mix which make it difficult to regulate what and when you feed your citrus.

Planting in Containers. Place prepared soil mix (with the bagged compost already mixed in) in the bottom of your container, about one-quarter of the way up. Gently slide the rootball out of the old container and shake off some of the old soil so that the roots will have easy access to the new soil mix. Use your fingers to spread the roots, but be careful not to break them off. It's best to repot a tree that has a slightly moist—not dry—root system. Place the loosened root mass into the new container and gently fill with the planting mix, packing down lightly to remove air spaces. Gently shake and tap the pot to settle, making sure it is centered and straight. The top of the rootball should be level or slightly above the surface of the soil. Water deeply two times in a row. Stake and loosely tie, if needed. The stake should be at least two to three inches away from the trunk of the tree.

It's a good idea to re-pot your young tree every few years or so, or if you notice that the soil level has settled down a couple of inches, exposing the crown of the rootball. Adding fresh soil and root-pruning will ensure the long-term health of your plant.

Watering Containers. Citrus trees require soil that is evenly moist but never soggy. Water before leaves show wilting. Check the moisture level in the soil by sticking your finger two inches down into the soil feeling for wetness. If it's dry or barely moist, then you know it's time to water.

Growing Indoors

For a lot of dedicated gardeners in cold winter regions, growing 'Meyer' lemons means moving potted plants to an indoor location to protect them from freezing temperatures—that, and adding a supplemental "grow light," and maybe even increasing the humidity with regular misting. Ask whether it's worth it and these gardeners will be quick to tell you what a rewarding activity it is, with the 'Meyer' lemons frequently providing sweet smelling blossoms and, if they're really lucky, maybe even some delicious fruit.

Light & Location. Indoor citrus trees will need as much sunlight as possible for healthy growth. Choose a south-facing window with unobstructed light for best results. If you are growing in a space with less than five hours of sunlight during the winter months, you'll need to supplement the lack of sunlight with full spectrum grow lights. T5 fluorescent bulbs in the 6500k color temperature are ideal for most indoor growing. To provide adequate light, lamps should be kept one to two feet above the trees at all times, which also prevents the lights from burning the foliage.

Temperature: Room temperatures of around 55°F to 85°F are ideal for indoor citrus growing. Do not to allow temperatures to fall lower than 32°F as this will start to cause problems for your tree. *Note:* As important as it is to provide moderate indoor temperatures, never place your citrus directly in the path of heat blown by a heating vent.

Humidity: The humidity level in the room is also very important for your tree's health. A common approach to this challenge is to elevate the pot on small river rocks or gravel in a saucer. This combined with misting the tree foliage with a spray bottle during those dry winter months will also help increase humidity. The goal is not to soak the tree, as this can encourage fungal growth, but to maintain a similar humidity to the outside world.

Soil and Water: The soil and water advice for growing citrus in containers indoors is the same for growing in containers outdoors. See pages 93 – 94).

Fertilization: You'll get the best results from using a fertilizer specifically formulated for citrus. These specialty products are available in different forms, from organic slow-release fertilizers, to dry fertilizers for top dressing and watering in, to liquid fertilizers to dilute with water. Which you choose is largely a matter of personal choice. Most importantly, read and follow all label instructions and do not be tempted to think "more is better," as too much fertilizer can damage or even kill plants. If any of your citrus are showing signs of chlorosis (yellowing leaves in one form or another), apply a specially formulated product containing chelated iron, zinc, and manganese. Read and follow all label instructions.

Pasta with Tuna and Fried Lemons, *continued from page 63*

3. In a well-salted pot of boiling water, cook pasta according to package directions until al dente. Drain and hold pasta in a colander.

4. In the same large skillet, heat the remaining 2 tablespoons olive oil over medium heat. Add garlic and the white parts of the scallions; cook until fragrant, about 1 minute. Add anchovies and green olives and cook until anchovies melt, 2 to 3 minutes longer. Add dry white wine and let it reduce by about half, then add cooked pasta and chopped parsley and toss well to coat. Add tuna and lemon triangles and toss well until heated through.

5. Scatter the red-pepper flakes, chopped green parts of the scallions and the toasted panko bread crumbs on top. Serve with lemon wedges on the side for squeezing.

Clam Fettucine, *continued from page 65*

3. Zest the lemon and then juice it. Reserve zest and juice separately.

4. Add the hot red pepper flakes to the pan and cook for 30 seconds; add the white wine and cook for 2-3 minutes or until slightly reduced. Add the reserved garlic and anchovies and just bring to a boil.

5. Add the pasta, clams, lemon juice, pepper and salt; mix with tongs, tossing until pasta is well-coated with sauce. Add reserved pasta water if pasta is too dry. Top with the parsley and celery leaves, toasted panko, lemon zest and a drizzle of olive oil and a sprinkle of salt. Good eating!

Amy's Roast 'Meyer' Chicken, *continued from page 69*

when pierced with the tip of a sharp knife at the thigh and an instant-read thermometer registers 165°F when inserted into the breast, after approximately 55 to 75 minutes of cooking.

4. When the chicken is done, transfer it to a serving platter, loosely tent with aluminum foil, and let rest for at least ten minutes before carving. Garnish each serving of sliced chicken with parsley and a lemon wedge, if desired. Save any garlic pieces for spreading on slices of toasted baguette.

Indoor Oven Instructions for Amy's Roast 'Meyer' Chicken

1. Preheat oven to 425°F.

2. Fold the wing tips under the back of the chicken, and place in a roasting pan not much larger than the chicken. Juice the lemons and pour over the chicken and inside the cavity. Generously salt and pepper the chicken inside and out. Make a bed of three sprigs of rosemary under the chicken and place one or two sprigs inside the cavity. Break the garlic head into cloves, smash them with the side of a knife and discard peels; and add a few to the cavity and the rest to the pan around the chicken. Rub the softened butter across the breasts and tops of drumsticks.

3. Roast for 20 minutes at 425°F. Reduce the heat to 350°F. and cook another 40 to 45 minutes. Check for doneness by piercing the thigh joint; the juices should run clear. Or insert a meat thermometer into the thickest part of the thigh; remove the bird from oven when thermometer registers 165°degrees. Loosely tent the chicken with aluminum foil and let rest for at least ten minutes before carving. Spoon pan drippings over the sliced chicken and serve immediately.

'Meyer' Lemon Curd, *continued from page 77*

coats the back of a spoon dipped into the mixture instead of running off.

7. Remove the pan from the heat and pour the thickened, still hot curd through a fine mesh sieve, pressing it into the bowl below, using the back of a large spoon or rubber spatula. Scrape the outside of the sieve, making sure not to leave any curd behind.

8. Immediately add the butter pats, one at a time, to the hot curd and stir until they fully melt. Once all the butter has been added, let the curd come to room temperaure and then seal by pressing plastic wrap gently onto the surface of the curd (this avoids a "skin" from forming). Set in the refrigerator for a few hours before using. Sealed, it will keep in the refrigerator for two weeks.

'Meyer' Lemon Shaker Pie, *continued from page 81*

5. Cut slits in the crust with a sharp knife, forming steam vents, and bake the pie in the middle of the oven for 25 minutes. Reduce the temperature to 350°F. and bake the pie for 20 to 25 minutes more, or until the crust is golden. Let the pie cool on a rack and serve warm.

1-2-3-4 Cake with 'Meyer' Lemon Curd Filling, *continued from page 87*

toothpick inserted in the center of the cake comes out clean. Cool on wire racks for ten minutes, then loosen from the pans and turn back out on the racks to cool completely.

5. Once the cake layers are cool, spread a generous layer of the reserved lemon curd between the two middle layers. Then frost with buttercream frosting (recipe below).

Buttercream Frosting

1 cup unsalted butter, softened, not melted
3-plus cups of powdered sugar (depending on the consistency desired)
¼ teaspoon salt
Approximately 4 tablespoons heavy cream (again, depending on the consistency desired)

Using a handheld electric mixer, beat the butter at medium speed for one minute. Turn off mixer and add 3 cups of powdered sugar and mix with butter at low speed until thoroughly mixed. Increase speed to medium. Add the vanilla, salt, and 2 tablespoons of the heavy cream. Beat for 2 to 3 minutes until the frosting is fluffy. Adjust the amount of additional cream or powdered sugar until you have the consistency you want.

Acknowledgements

Many thanks to Patty and her amazingly productive 'Meyer' lemon bush and all the lemons it provided for many of the recipes in this book—not to mention the lemon marmalade she/it produced like magic at the last minute. Throughout the process of writing this book, Amy has been not only a culinary inspiration but a contributor of recipes and good advice—thank you Amy, for your talent and willingness to share. And to Mike for his bonhomie and deep experience in all things culinary. Thanks also to Saul and Karen for pitching in in both the kitchen and at the dining room table; it's good to have fun while you work! And it's good to have friends like Lance who emails you right back when you have even the most esoteric of questions, not to mention the kind folks at the legendary Four Winds Growers who know as much about 'Meyer' lemons (and any other citrus you can think of) as anyone out there. Last but hardly least, thank you Michèle for your peerless editorial skills and for keeping me from stumbling over myself in the English Department. Thanks to all of you for your cheerful assistance.

• • •

A couple of quick explanations concerning single quotation marks and salt—plain salt: First, I felt the need answer the question as to why there are single quotation marks around the name 'Meyer'—a practice that confuses some readers and annoys others. Botanical nomenclature is, at best, complex and confusing, so without going into too much detail, single quotes around a name indicates that the plant is a cultivar (short for "cultivated variety"), distinct from the general species. Any more of a detailed explanation would go on for pages so, hopefully, enough said. As for the decision to keep "salt" as just salt in the recipes, with no modifiers like kosher or sea or any of the other types available, it was made in an attempt to keep the ingredient information simple and consistent. It also recognizes that most home cooks use the salt they are used to and have on hand and leave it at that.

One of my favorites from my grandfather's collection. I'm not quite sure how, but this one—thankfully—survived the big earthquake of August 2014 here in Napa.

A Note on the Illustrations

As a resource for the paintings in this book, I had the good fortune of inheriting two generations' worth of blue-and-white Chinese and Japanese porcelain. Both my grandfather, Captain Nels A. Sinnes and my father, Captain Alfred E. Sinnes, spent decades in the Far East during their service in the Merchant Marines. Virtually all of the pieces were presented to them as gifts when they arrived at one port or another, some of them dating back to the 1920s. It seemed a natural combination—that a citrus found in Asia should be painted on Asian porcelain. What a pleasure to make this project a multi-generational voyage with a couple of great mates I had the pleasure of calling "Grandpa" and "Dad."

• • •

In working on this book, I debated whether to include only paintings painted specifically for this book, or to include paintings done prior to when the idea for this book had even occurred to me. In

My grandfather, Capt. Nels Sinnes, aboard the S.S. Samoa, *December 1941, shortly before being torpedoed by a Japanese submarine off the coast of Cape Mendocino, California—but that's another story…*

My father, Capt. Alfred Sinnes, arriving Singapore from Manila, S.S. Idaho, *Voyage 47W. States Steamship Company. December 18, 1977.*

the end, I decided to include some of the earlier paintings as I thought a progression would be more interesting—especially considering that I started using oil paints and moved to watercolors and then to gouache, as time went on.

I have been both influenced and inspired by the English artist (living in France), Julian Merrow-Smith. He was one of the originators of the "painting-a-day" movement and remains one of its best practitioners. His beautiful work can be seen at www.shiftinglight.com.

I did virtually all of my painting at the kitchen table in my old house in the Old Town section of Napa. I've tried other locations, but I always gravitate back to the kitchen. It's not very convenient—especially when I want to play cards, or eat a meal, or any of the other things one normally does at a kitchen table. But it's homey and warm, the light is good, and with NPR on the radio, quite companionable.

For whatever reason, I find it almost impossible to paint anywhere other than my kitchen table. Go figure. The windows face south and east, resulting in some very strong sunshine—and equally strong shadow patterns—across the table.

Index

www.ingramcontent.com/pod-product-compliance
Lightning Source LLC
LaVergne TN
LVHW021134160826
845679LV00016B/1742

* 9 7 9 8 2 3 4 0 0 4 0 2 4 *